Just Roll with it

Recipes For Easy Embossed Cookies

By Stacy Krems
Edited by Carol Johnson

The Homestead Press

Table of Contents

Grandma Dorothy

Dedication:

This cookbook is dedicated to my late grandmother Dorothy. What I would do to just sit at the kitchen table with you, just once more. To my husband Kurt who keeps me laughing. To my daughter Izzy who inspires me everyday. To my parents, Don & Boise, who are my biggest cheerleaders!

Acknowledgements:

To my friend and publisher, Emily Kitching whose patience, humility, and kindness inspires me every day to be a better person. To my illustrator, Katie Overgard—her ability to climb in my head to turn my thoughts into charming images is astonishing.

Introduction

The earliest summers that I can remember are the ones that I spent in a tiny, one-stop-sign type town in western Colorado with my grandparents. In the height of summer we'd do anything from fishing in near-by mosquito-infested waters to making fruit roll ups in the backyard to picking Palisade peaches on Sundays. If I was lucky, I'd pick the longest cucumber my grandparents "had ever seen" or get even luckier and walk up to the post office with my grandpa and eat a secret donut on the way back home. Shhh, grandma never knew.

My strongest and most cherished memory was spending hours upon hours at the kitchen table watching my grandma bake. With curlers in her hair, cigarette in one hand, and a tub of Crisco in the other, my grandmother would whip up some of this and some of that as I watched her every move. It was in these hours that we just talked. She talked and I listened. I talked and she listened. All the while, she baked and I watched.

This seemingly boring time of just sitting at the kitchen table turned into the greatest gift for me. As grandmothers often do, my grandmother taught by showing. She showed me that spending time with someone you love is the best time there is. So what if the pistachio pudding is a bit runny, does

it matter? Who cares if the donuts were too mushy…no big deal. And if the bacon is too crispy for Papa's favorite BLT sandwich, does it really matter? We were busy doing important things…like being together.

There are people around you who simply want to be with you. They don't want the latest and greatest gadget, a pretty sweater, or even a pack of gum. They just want to be with you.

There is someone who is excited to just sit, be with you, and watch you do whatever it is that you do. Little will you know that those moments together may be etched in their minds and become cherished memories. Go get those people and bring them into the kitchen.

Our rolling pins can help you to make beautiful memories because they are so much more than what they can physically create. Yes, you can create beautiful cookies and even be the star in your neighborhood cookie exchange. But more than being just utilitarian, our rolling pins are symbolic. They represent time, an experience, and something heartfelt. There are moments in life that matter, and often times they happen without our even knowing. With our rolling pins, you, your family, and your friends will know that you have created something special.

Why Rolling Pins?

This sweet book is filled with fun & easy recipes as well as providing little moments for you to enjoy along the way.

Our rolling pins originated in Colorado, circa 2015! I'm often asked how in the world I got started in the land of rolling pins. Well, I blame my husband for this one. Kurt, my husband, is a master of all things technical, and he loves tools—the more complex the better. For years he talked about purchasing a laser engraver, and for years I pretended I wasn't listening. Then one day I guess I cracked...and said "yes." Little did I know that this laser engraver would become the epicenter of our world and change our lives for the better.

Here we are with this massive machine...what were we going to make? That was the million dollar question. I love to bake, and Kurt understood the various elements of wood—so why not try a rolling pin? It was more of a shot in the dark than anything, but we had to make something.

Our conversation went like this: Hmm. What would be the most unique thing to see on a rolling pin? We love dogs; do other people like dogs? No, I think more people like cats. Let's design a cat rolling pin. Who's going to design it? Oh, me? No, you? Where do I even get a cat file, and how do I design this?

Sweet Rolling Pins

Somehow, some way, one of us designed our very first Cat rolling pin, and, boy…our family went from loving dogs to loving cats!

Within months of having this new machine, we found ourselves working around the clock as we fulfilled orders for over 2,000 cat-themed rolling pins. We learned a couple of valuable lessons from this experience: people love cats and people love baking. We worked in shifts as our machine was running around the clock. It was exciting, exhausting, frustrating, exhilarating—and a crash course in learning. As a side note, this is an amazing example to just begin. Start from wherever you are. You hear those words in personal development seminars or on bumper stickers, and it's true! Even if you don't know what you're doing…just start!

Fast forward to today. We now have a dedicated workshop outside of our home housing various machines that we use in creating our rolling pins. It's a family-run business where often times you'll see my parents preparing the rolling pins for use, our daughter threading recipes through twine, and my husband helping with the technical side. Our two bulldogs help as assistants, too.

What Is a Rolling Pin?

According to a Google search, it's believed that rolling pins were first used by the Etruscan civilization in ancient Italy from around 800 BC and were used to flatten dough.

Even in writing that last sentence, that fact is amazing to me. There exists a tool in our 21st-century kitchens which is believed to have been created so long ago and is still being used today! To think that for centuries, a rolling pin was used in various states of kitchens to create something for families or friends...be it bread, a pastry, a cookie, etc. That's pretty amazing that a tradition of using a tool is so old. There's even some romance to that.

While rolling pins have evolved over thousands of years, the most traditional rolling pin you'll see today has a long wooden barrel between two handles, and their main function is to roll dough to a flattened thinness. There are a variety of styles of rolling pins from those with handles to some with no handles, tapered wooden barrels to non-tapered, and engraved to non-engraved. They can be made out of wood, porcelain, glass, and even acrylic. The Japanese use a rolling pin at least 20 inches wide to make Udon noodles, and you see a four-inch-wide rolling pin sometimes used by potters.

The main purposes of our rolling pins is for homemade cookies, fondant, pottery, and flour ornaments...but sometimes they are handy in a sword fight or for use as a back roller.

We knew right away that we were going to make laser-engraved rolling pins which means we cut specific designs into the wood—from dogs, sugar skulls, and company logos to holiday trees and beautiful floral designs. Sometimes we hire designers to create beautiful custom designs, and sometimes we get lucky and design them ourselves.

How to Use our Rolling Pins

Next to each recipe, you'll see an image with three rolling pins that say, "'less intricate, intricate and/or more intricate." We designed this key to point out the best suited rolling pin(s) for each recipe. You'll find some recipes have dough that is thick and grainier where using a rolling pin with a wider design is best suited. For this, we recommend using a "less intricate" type of rolling pin. Or you'll find another recipe with dough that feels thinner, contains finer ingredients where using a "more intricate" rolling pin would be best. This pin contains a lot of details and is very intricate.

Once you roll out your dough to desired thickness with a smooth rolling pin, dust engraved rolling pin with flour. Then, using moderate pressure roll over dough. Helpful hint, rather than using the handles on the engraved pin use the palms of your hands to roll the wooden barrel.

Rolling pin design guide.

"Snowflakes" Rolling Pin

Purpose AND Care Instructions

With our sweet rolling pins you can make a variety of adorable, fun, and beautiful cookies. Although we originally thought they would be used in baking with homemade roll out cookies and fondant, we soon realized they're actually a multi-use tool. You can also use them for pottery texture, for kitchen décor, or even for salt and flour ornaments. They're practical, unique, and a definite conversation starter!

After each use, rinse in hot water. For tricky areas, use a toothbrush. No soap necessary and let air dry. Not intended for store-bought dough or homemade pie crust. (Why? See page 71)

"Dala Horse" Rolling Pin

Equipment List

1. Regular rolling pin

2. Engraved rolling pin

3. Pastry brush

4. Small bowl of flour

5. Measuring cups and measuring spoons

6. Standing mixer (preferred), hand-held mixer or heavy
   wooden spoon

7. Rubber spatula

8. Cookie cutter or drinking glass

9. Parchment paper

10. Cookie sheets

11. Cooling rack

12. Timer

13. Refrigerator

14. Oven mitt or hand towel

15. Spatula

16. Food coloring

17. Piping tips (for decorating and for cutting out small
    pieces of dough)

Measure Equivalents

Cup	=	Fluid OZ	=	TBSP	=	TSP
1 C		8 oz		16 Tbsp		48 tsp
3/4 C		6 oz		12 Tbsp		36 tsp
2/3 C		5 oz		11 Tbsp		32 tsp
1/2 C		4 oz		8 Tbsp		24 tsp
1/3 C		3 oz		5 Tbsp		16 tsp
1/4 C		2 oz		4 Tbsp		12 tsp
1/8 C		1 oz		2 Tbsp		6 tsp
1/16 C		.5 oz		1 Tbsp		3 tsp

Basic Ingredients

(See recipes for additional ingredients.)

1. Unsalted Butter (room temperature)
2. Granulated Sugar
3. Brown Sugar
4. Unbleached Flour
5. Salt
6. Baking Powder
7. Baking Soda
8. Vanilla Extract

Allergies Disclaimer

All recipes included here assume we all have tummies of steel. As you are aware of your own health and any allergies, please make alterations or substitutions as needed.

Tips for Rolling & Cutting Cookies

Just as you may have a best friend in life, someone you love to talk to, grab coffee with, or share your silliest secrets with—your go-to friend—you go hand-in-hand, right? The same applies to flour and the engraved rolling pin. They're best friends and they love being together. Keep this cute thought in mind when you're rolling out the dough and make sure the rolling pin is generously dusted with flour before it even hits the dough.

Work surface: To prepare your work and rolling surface, you have a few choices. The main intention of this step is to prevent the dough from sticking to anything and to eliminate adding excess flour to the dough (this will result in stiff dough.) My preference is to cut a small piece of parchment paper and place my dough on top of it. I lightly dust my solid rolling pin with flour and roll the dough. The parchment creates a "lazy Susan" effect as I'm able to spin the parchment paper around on the counter to position it the way I want. Some people prefer to create a sandwich: parchment paper, dough, then cover with an additional piece of parchment paper. Other bakers prefer to use just the counter or even a thin cutting board. You choose what works for you!

Work with cool dough: Dough loves being cold, and having it cold serves a great purpose. Using cold dough lets your cookies maintain their shape better. Not only do I refrigerate the dough in disc shapes (wrapped snug as a bug in parchment paper and aluminum foil), once I roll out the dough I then place the raw cookies on cookie sheets and place the cookie sheets back in the refrigerator again for about 10 more minutes or while the other cookies are in the oven.

Work in small portions: Using a small portion of dough gives you more control and is less overwhelming. When I work with one disc, I usually break that down even further and use ½ of the dough at a time, sometimes even less.

Flour your rolling pin: If you remember anything, it's this: before each pass of your engraved rolling pin, make sure to generously dust your rolling pin with flour. This prevents the dough from sticking to the rolling pin and makes cleaning the pin easy. Remember, flour and the engraved rolling pin are besties so make 'em happy!

"Chili Peppers" Rolling Pin

Recipes

Sugar Cookies

- 1 cup butter (room temp)
- 1 cup granulated sugar
- 1 egg slightly beaten
- 3 tsp vanilla
- 1 tsp baking powder
- 3 cups flour

Directions:

Blend butter and sugar until creamy. Beat in egg and vanilla. Fold in dry ingredients until just combined. Do not over mix. Divide the dough in half, shaping the dough into two discs. (Working with a smaller portion size is much easier than working with the entire recipe.) Wrap each disc in Tupperware, plastic wrap, or parchment paper wrapped in tin foil and place in the refrigerator for 1 hour. Remove from refrigerator and work with one disc at a time.

With a plain rolling pin, roll the dough to your desired thickness. I enjoy 1/8 of an inch thick. Dip your pastry brush in flour and dust the entire surface of the engraved rolling pin. (Remember flour and rolling pin are best friends.) Using moderate pressure, roll over the dough with engraved rolling pin until the image appears. Cut out desired shapes with a cookie cutter or drinking glass. Place cookies on cookie sheets that are lined with parchment paper.

Thoughts:

This is such a simple recipe that loves to be a trusty staple and classic. But sometimes we might put on a little lipstick to fancy ourselves up. To add some fun to this recipe, add in lemon extract, orange extract, anise, or even rum extract. For starters, add 1 tsp of one extract per recipe. Over time you may find you like combining two flavors together, etc. Or add in the full zest of a lemon or orange for not only a new flavor but also a new texture in your cookies.

Bake 350 F for 7-10 minutes or until the outside of cookies turn slight brown.

Cookie credit: The Cookie Cutter Shop

Suggested rolling pin: "less intricate, intricate"

intricate

less intricate

more intricate

"Nordic Animals" Rolling Pin

Conversation Starters....

"Do you remember when...?"

Springerle Shortbread

- 1 cup butter (room temp)
- ½ cup packed light brown sugar
- 2 tsp granulated sugar
- ½ tsp salt
- 1 large egg
- 1 tsp vanilla
- 3 cups King Arthur Unbleached All Purpose Flour

Directions:

Beat together the butter, sugars, and salt until light and creamy. Beat in egg and vanilla. Fold in the flour until just combined. Do not over mix the flour. Divide the dough in half, shaping the dough into two discs. (Working with a smaller portion size is much easier than working with the entire recipe.) Wrap each disc in Tupperware, plastic wrap, or parchment paper wrapped in tin foil and place in the refrigerator for 1 hour. Remove from refrigerator and work with one disc at a time.

With a plain rolling pin, roll the dough to your desired thickness. I enjoy 1/8 of an inch thick. Dip your pastry brush in flour and dust the entire surface of the engraved rolling pin. (Remember flour and rolling pin are best friends.) Using moderate pressure, roll over the dough with engraved rolling pin until the image appears. Cut out desired shapes with a cookie cutter or drinking glass. Place cookies on cookie sheets that are lined with parchment paper.

Thoughts:

This is tea towels down, my favorite recipe of all time! It's easy, not so sweet, and so versatile. From changing the flavors with extracts, adding in fruit peels, and even nuts, it's the most dependable recipe I've found to date.

I love baking with materials I have on hand and sometimes I'm just lazy. I was walking down the baking aisle and noticed all the pre-packaged drink mixes: tea, hot chocolate, apple cider, etc. Toss some of these into your cookies for easy variations. Just remember, this is a fantastic staple recipe to start from!

Extracts are an amazing addition to change the flavor of this recipe. From lemon, orange, rum, almond, to peppermint—just a few drops creates a new cookie.

Bake 350 F for 9-11 minutes or until the outside of cookies turn slight brown.

Cookie credit: King Arthur Flour

Suggested rolling pin type: "less intricate, intricate, more intricate"

intricate

less intricate

more intricate

15

Windowpane Cookies

• Hard candies (such as a Jolly Rancher, smashed into small pieces)

• See **Springerle Shortbread** recipe and make as described.

Directions:

Make Springerle Shortbread cookie recipe as described up until you roll out the dough.

With a plain rolling pin, roll the dough to your desired thickness. I enjoy 1/8 of an inch thick. Dip your pastry brush in flour and dust the entire surface of the engraved rolling pin. (Remember flour and rolling pin are best friends.) Using moderate pressure, roll over the dough with engraved rolling pin until the image appears. Cut out desired shapes with a cookie cutter or drinking glass. Using a smaller cookie cutter or even a piping tip, cut out an additional space in the middle of the cookie. Place cookies on cookie sheets that are lined with parchment paper.

Unwrap the hard candies from their plastic wrapper and put aside in a larger, plastic bag. Using a small mallet or rolling pin, smash the hard candies until they become as small as you can get them.

"Paisley" Rolling Pin

Sprinkle 1 tsp of the hard candy dust into the middle hole of the cookie. Bake 350 F for 9-11 minutes or until the outside of cookies turn slight brown. You'll see the hard candy bubble up and melt. Once removed from the oven, let sit for at least 10 minutes before you move the cookies. Note, the hard candy will be hot, so use caution. Also remember you'll be biting into a hard candy so if your teeth need extra love, you might just want to suck on the piece of hard candy. Because these are such beautiful cookies, some folks pop a hole in the cookies and hang them on a tree or adorn their gingerbread houses with them.

Cookie credit: King Arthur Flour

"Floral Swirl" Rolling Pin

Conversation Starters....

"What's something I say all the time?"

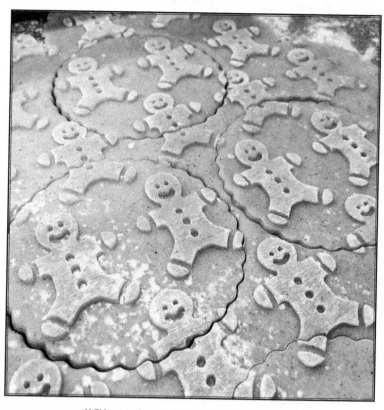

"Gingerbread Man" Rolling Pin

Gingerbread Cookies

- 1 cup butter (room temp)
- 1 cup granulated sugar
- 1 egg
- 1 cup molasses
- 2 tsp ginger
- 1 tsp cinnamon
- 1 tsp ground cloves
- ½ tsp salt
- 5 cups flour
- 1 ½ tsp baking soda

Directions:

Beat together the butter and sugar until light and creamy. Beat in egg and molasses. Sift together all dry ingredients and gradually add into wet mixture. Fold in dry ingredients until just combined. Do not over mix the flour. (Note: Take a moment to pause here. How divine does your kitchen smell right now?) Divide the dough in half, shaping the dough into two discs. (Working with a smaller portion size is much easier than working with the entire recipe.) Wrap each disc in Tupperware, plastic wrap or parchment paper wrapped in tin foil and place in the refrigerator for 1 hour. Remove from refrigerator and work with one disc at a time.

Because this recipe makes a lot of dough, take that one disc you're working with and divide that into ½ or even ¼. Or find the amount of dough that seems manageable to you.

IMPORTANT RECIPE NOTES

With a plain rolling pin, roll the dough to your desired thickness. For this recipe, I enjoy 1/4 - 1/8 of an inch thick. Dip your pastry brush in flour and dust the entire surface of the engraved rolling pin. (Remember flour and rolling pin are best friends.) Using moderate pressure, roll over the dough with engraved rolling pin until the image appears. Cut out desired shapes with a cookie cutter or drinking glass. Place cookies on cookie sheets that are lined with parchment paper.

Thoughts:

I love this recipe because it makes your kitchen smell so inviting and cozy. In addition to "bringing the holidays into your kitchen," this recipe is fantastic for making cookies that showcase the design of the rolling pin. But can I offer even better news? This dough is sturdy enough to build ginger-bread houses, sleighs, and other fun centerpieces that require strong walls!

Bake 350 F for 9-11 minutes or until the outside of cookies turn slight brown. If baking larger cookies for a gingerbread house, bake 2-3 minutes longer, about 12-14 minutes, until the sides turn a slight brown. Cool completely before you begin construction.

Cookie credit: Sweet Anna Jean (Salida, Colo.)

Suggested rolling pin type: "less intricate"

Peanut Butter Roll Out Cookies

- ½ cup creamy peanut butter
- ¾ cup butter (room temp)
- 1 cup packed brown sugar
- ½ cup granulated sugar
- 2 eggs
- ¼ tsp salt
- ½ tsp baking powder
- 3 – 3 ½ cups flour

Directions:

Beat together the peanut butter, softened butter, both sugars and eggs until creamy and blended. In separate bowl, combine the salt, baking soda, and flour and mix until combined. Slowly fold the dry ingredients into wet ingredients until the dough begins to pull away from the side of the mixing bowl.

Divide the dough in half, shaping the dough into two discs. (Working with a smaller portion size is much easier than working with the entire recipe.) Wrap each disc in Tupperware, plastic wrap or parchment paper wrapped in tin foil and place in the refrigerator for 1 hour. Remove from refrigerator and work with one disc at a time.

With a plain rolling pin, roll the dough to your desired thickness. I enjoy 1/4 of an inch thick for this recipe. Dip your pastry brush in flour and dust the entire surface of the engraved rolling pin. (Remember flour and rolling pin are best friends.) Using moderate pressure, roll over the dough with engraved rolling pin until the image appears. Cut out desired shapes with a cookie cutter or drinking glass. Place cookies on cookie sheets lined with parchment paper.

Thoughts:

The peanut butter adds a bit of texture to your cookies so I recommend using an engraved rolling pin with a thick design.

Bake 350F for 7-10 minutes.

Cookie credit: Sister-in-Law

Suggested rolling pin type: "less intricate"

Chai Cookies

See **Springerle Shortbread** recipe and make as described. The only alteration is to add the Chai spices below in with the flour.

- ½ tsp salt
- 2 tsp. cinnamon
- 1 tsp. cardamom
- 1 tsp ginger
- ½ tsp allspice
- ½ ground cloves

Thoughts:

Once again, the Springerle Shortbread recipe is a baker's favorite. This light and subtle flavor of Indian spices just begs for a cup of tea!

Suggested rolling pin: "less intricate, intricate, more intricate"

intricate

less intricate

more intricate

"The Homestead" Rolling Pin Design

Conversation Starters....

"Did I ever tell you...?"

Hot Chocolate Roll Out Cookies

- 1 cup butter (room temp)
- ½ cup granulated sugar
- ½ cup packed light brown sugar
- 1 egg
- 3 packets of powdered hot chocolate mix (appx ¾ cup)
- 1 ½ tsp vanilla
- 2 ½ cups flour
- ½ cup miniature chocolate chips (optional)
- ½ cup miniature marsh bellow bits (optional)

Directions:

Beat together the butter and sugars until creamy. Beat in egg and vanilla. In a separate bowl, combine the flour and hot chocolate mix until combined. Fold in the flour and hot chocolate mixture into wet mixture until just combined. Do not over mix. Add the chocolate chips and marshmallows if desired. (Note: by adding the chocolate and marshmallows, your end cookie will have more texture and be less smooth. This will result in a less "finished" cookie, but it sure will taste good!)

Divide the dough in half, shaping the dough into two discs. (Working with smaller portion sizes is much easier than working with the entire recipe at once.) Wrap each disc in Tupperware, plastic wrap, or parchment paper wrapped in tin foil and place in the refrigerator for 1 hour. Remove from refrigerator and work with one disc at a time.

With a plain rolling pin, roll the dough to your desired thickness. I enjoy 1/8 of an inch thick but you can roll to 1/4 inch. Dip your pastry brush in flour and dust the entire surface of the engraved rolling pin. (Remember flour and rolling pin are best friends.) Using moderate pressure, roll over the dough with engraved rolling pin until the image appears. Cut out desired shapes with a cookie cutter or drinking glass. Place cookies on cookie sheets that are lined with parchment paper.

Thoughts:

Have you heard that some people add in chili powder to hot chocolate to give it kick? Or even chipotle powder or cayenne pepper?

Bake 375 F for 7-9 minutes or until the outside of cookies turn slight brown.

Recipe adapted from, I BAKE YOU BAKE.

Suggested rolling pin: "less intricate, intricate"

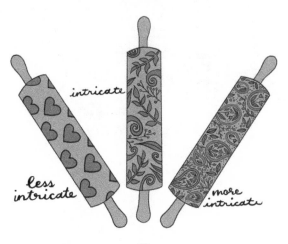

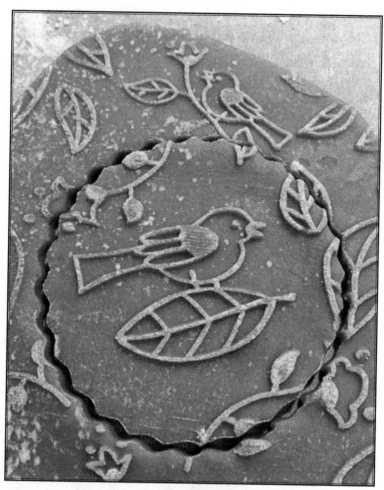

"Li'l Birdies" Rolling Pin

Conversation Starters....

"Let me tell you when..."

Chocolate Chipotle Cookies

- 5 cups all-purpose flour
- 1 cup cocoa powder
- 2 tsp espresso powder (optional)
- 1 tsp salt
- 2 tsp cinnamon
- 1 tsp ground chipotle chili powder
- 2 cups butter, (room temp)
- 2 cups granulated sugar
- 2 large eggs
- 2 tsp vanilla

Directions:

Combine flour, salt, and spices in bowl and set aside. In large mixing bowl, cream butter and sugar until light and fluffy. Beat in egg and vanilla until well combined. Gradually add the flour mixture at low speed. Remember to scrape down those sides to incorporate all the dough!

Divide the dough in half, shaping the dough into two discs. (Working with smaller portion sizes is much easier than working with the entire recipe at once.) Wrap each disc in Tupperware, plastic wrap, or parchment paper wrapped in tin foil and place in the refrigerator for 1 hour. Remove from refrigerator and work with one disc at a time.

With a plain rolling pin, roll the dough to your desired thickness. I enjoy 1/8 of an inch thick but you can roll to ¼ inch. Dip your pastry brush in flour and dust the entire surface of the engraved rolling pin. (Remember flour and rolling pin are best friends.) Using moderate pressure, roll over the dough with engraved rolling pin until the image appears. Cut out desired shapes with a cookie cutter or drinking glass. Place cookies on cookie sheets that are lined with parchment paper.

Bake 350 for 8-12 minutes.

Suggested rolling pin: "less intricate, intricate"

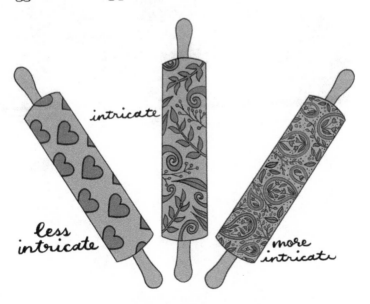

"Floral Rooster" Rolling Pin

Conversation
Starters....

"If I were a kitchen utensil, what would I be?"

Lime AND Coconut Cookies

- 2 cups all-purpose flour
- 1 cup butter (room temp)
- ½ granulated sugar
- ½ tsp salt
- 1 tsp vanilla
- 2 tsp Key Lime juice (optional)
- ½ cup coconut, shredded and toasted
- Zest of two limes (add more if you want that tart tingle in your cheeks)

Directions:

Blend sugar, lime zest, coconut, and vanilla in food processor and continue to pulse until finely chopped. With regular rolling pin, roll the dough to your desired thickness. I enjoy 1/4 − 1/8 inch thick for this recipe. Dip your pastry brush in flour and dust the entire surface of the engraved rolling pin. (Remember flour and rolling pin are best friends.) Using moderate pressure, roll over the dough with engraved rolling pin until the image appears. Cut out desired shapes with a cookie cutter or drinking glass. Place cookies on cookie sheets that are lined with parchment paper.

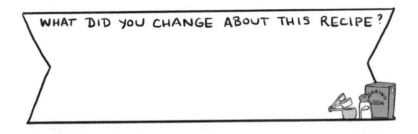

Thoughts:

This dough will have some texture with pretty green specks of lime. The flavor of this cookie is really mild so feel free to add more zest or key lime juice to get that pucker effect!

Bake 350 F for 8-10 minutes.

Cookie credit: Top 50 Shortbread Recipes,
Julie Brooke

Suggested rolling pin: "less intricate, intricate"

intricate

less
intricate

more
intricate

"Regal Animals" Rolling Pin

Conversation Starters....

"Tell me about your..."

3-Ingredient Nutella Cookies

- 1 cup all-purpose flour
- 1 cup Nutella
- 1 large egg

Directions:

Blend all three ingredients together until well combined. With a plain rolling pin, roll the dough to your desired thickness. I enjoy 1/4 – 1/8 inch thick for this recipe. Dip your pastry brush in flour and dust the entire surface of the engraved rolling pin. (Remember flour and rolling pin are best friends.) Using moderate pressure, roll over the dough with engraved rolling pin until the image appears. Cut out desired shapes with a cookie cutter or drinking glass. Place cookies on cookie sheets that are lined with parchment paper.

Thoughts:

This dough resembles that of the peanut butter recipe in that it will appear a bit grainy when rolled out. You may notice you didn't have to pop this dough in the refrigerator. It wouldn't hurt if you did, but considering it makes such a small batch, I make the cookies right away and it works great.

Bake 350 F for 8-10 minutes.

Cookie credit: Gemma's Bigger Bolder Baking

Suggested rolling pin: "less intricate"

"Succulents" Rolling Pin

Conversation Starters....

"What would you think if..."

...IMPORTANT RECIPE NOTES...

S'more Graham Cracker Cookie

- ½ cup butter (room temp)
- ½ packed light brown sugar
- ¼ cup granulated sugar
- 1 egg
- 2 tsp honey
- ½ tsp vanilla
- 2 cups flour
- ¾ cup graham cracker crumbs (use food processor to chop as fine as possible)
- ¼ tsp baking soda
- ½ tsp salt

Directions:

Beat together the butter and sugars until creamy. Add egg, honey, and vanilla and continue to mix until well blended. Add flour, crumbs of graham crackers, baking soda, and salt and beat at low speed until well mixed. (Note: Yes, it's an extra step but finely chopping up the graham crackers is a must. Just when you think the little crumbs are fine, press that pulse button again on your food processor. The finer the crumbs, the smoother the cookie will be at the end. Work for it, baby!)

Divide the dough in half, shaping the dough into two discs. (Working with a smaller portion size is much easier than working with the entire recipe at once.) Wrap each disc in Tupperware, plastic wrap, or parchment paper wrapped in tin foil and place in the refrigerator for 1 hour. Remove from refrigerator and work with one disc at a time.

With a plain rolling pin, roll the dough to your desired thickness. I enjoy 1/8 of an inch thick. Dip your pastry brush in flour and dust the entire surface of the engraved rolling pin. (Remember flour and rolling pin are best friends.) Using moderate pressure, roll over the dough with engraved rolling pin until the image appears. Cut out desired shapes with a cookie cutter or drinking glass. Place cookies on cookie sheets that are lined with parchment paper.

Bake 350 F for 9-11 minutes or until the outside of cookies turn slight brown.

Suggested rolling pin: "less intricate"

intricate

less
intricate

more
intricate

Once the graham cracker cookies have cooled, grab your marshmallows and chocolate as it's S'mores time! There are two ways to use your cookies, so it's up to you.

#1- Oven:

Preheat oven to 350 degrees. Line cookies with the design facing the cookie sheet. Add one marshmallow and desired chocolate. Place in oven for 2-3 minutes. The marshmallow and chocolate will melt quickly so don't walk away! Remove from oven, place another cookie on top of the marshmallow-and-chocolate yumminess and squish the cookie down to create a S'mores!

#2 – Microwave:

Take small amount of chocolate and place in microwave-safe bowl. In small bursts of time, melt the chocolate until it becomes a spread. Set aside. Place a cookie with the design facing the plate. Add one marshmallow on top. Microwave for 10 seconds and watch that marshmallow fluff it's feathers and get fat. (If you've never seen a marshmallow in a microwave, you're in for a funny treat. They expand and will create a sticky mess if not watched.) Once your marshmallow is fat and happy, remove from microwave and set up your assembly line. Take another cookie with the design facing down and spread the melted chocolate on it. Place the chocolate side down on top of the fluffy marshmallow cookie. Squish together and enjoy!

Recipe adapted from Land O'Lakes

Springerle

- 4 large eggs, room temp
- 2 cups granulated sugar
- 1 ½ tbsp butter, room temp
- 1 tbsp baking powder
- 1 tsp anise extract
- 4 cups all-purpose flour

Directions:

This recipe is unlike any recipe you've ever made. Be sure to read this entire recipe before you start, as this beauty will take you two days to create from start to finish.

In large mixing bowl, beat eggs on high until fluffy. Add sugar, butter, and baking powder: beat on high speed for 15 minutes, scraping side occasionally. Beat in anise extract. Gradually add flour until well mixed. On floured surface, knead small portion of dough until manageable, as you will find this dough sticky!

With a plain rolling pin, roll the dough to your desired thickness. I enjoy 1/8 inch thick for this recipe. Dip your pastry brush in flour and dust the entire surface of the engraved rolling pin. (Remember flour and rolling pin are best friends.) Using moderate pressure, roll over the dough with engraved rolling pin until the image appears.

Cut into desired shapes and let sit on parchment-lined cookie sheets for 24 hours. Yup, let them air dry for 24 hours. You may be asking…but there are eggs in the dough and I need to put them in the fridge? Nope. Let them hang out on the kitchen table overnight, and in the morning you'll be able to feel that they're dry. This is what you're looking for.

Thoughts:

For me, this is a very difficult recipe to make because it takes a lot of patience and generally feels counterintuitive to what I typically bake. Springerle cookies are airy and light and showcase the design of the rolling pin magnificently. To me, this type of cookie resembles glass and creates absolutely beautiful cookies.

Bake 350 F in middle rack for 10 minutes. You will not see much browning of the cookie, so you'll need to pay attention to your timer versus gauging if the cookie is done by its color.

Suggested rolling pin: "less intricate, intricate, more intricate"

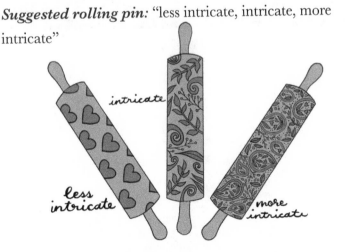

"Whimsy Tree" Rolling Pin

Homemade Cookie Butter

- 2 cups cookie crumbs (use any cookie you want)
- ¼ cup butter
- ½ cup sweetened condensed milk

Directions:

Add cookies to a food processor and pulse until the cookies become fine crumbs. In a small saucepan melt butter over medium heat. Stir in condensed milk until combined. Pour mixture into the food processor and pulse until well combined. Store in refrigerator for up to 1 week.

Thoughts:

If you're not satisfied with the cookies you just made, not to worry! Turn them into a yummy spread for croissants or toast or even for topping to an ice cream.

Cookie Butter credit: The Domestic Geek

"Goofy Reindeer" Rolling Pin

Chocolate Chip Cookie Dip

- ½ cup unsalted butter, room temp
- 1 (8 oz) package cream cheese, room temp
- 1/3 cup granulated sugar
- ¼ cup packed light brown sugar
- 2 ½ tsp vanilla extract
- ½ tsp salt
- 1 ½ cups semisweet chocolate chips
- Pretzels, fruit, vanilla wafers, crackers for dipping

Directions:

Cream butter, cream cheese, and sugars until smooth. Add in salt and extract and cream again until smooth. Stir in chocolate chips and spoon into a serving bowl. Serve with graham crackers, vanilla wafers, animal crackers, fruit, and pretzels.

Thoughts:

On a hot day when you don't want to turn your oven on, whip up this goodness and dip away. How much better can it get?

Recipe credit: JUST A TASTE

White Chocolate
Marshmallow Fondant

- 16 ounces mini marshmallows
- 2 tbsp water
- 2 tbsp light corn syrup (Karo)
- 1.5 -2 pounds powdered sugar (sifted)
- 2 ounces white chocolate or white candy melts (melted and slightly cooled)
- ½ cup white vegetable shortening (Crisco)

Directions:

In a large glass mixing bowl, add marshmallows and water. Microwave on high for 1 minute. Stir marshmallows with a spoon dipped in Crisco. Place back in microwave for 1 additional minute. Add corn syrup to melted marshmallows and stir until completely cooled. Slowly add in sifted powdered sugar, stirring frequently. When mixture gets too stiff to stir with a spoon, pour mixture onto a counter top that has been generously greased with Crisco. Finish kneading in the sifted powdered sugar. (Tip: Scoop some Crisco into your hands before kneading to prevent the fondant from sticking.)

You may or may not have to use all of the powdered sugar. It should be pliable but not so stiff that it is dry and difficult to knead. Melt the white chocolate or white candy melts in the microwave for 1 minute. Stir and continue to microwave in 15-second intervals until just melted. Don't overheat! Pour the melted and cooled white chocolate onto your fondant mixture on the counter and continue to knead until it's completely smooth. Form it into a ball; lightly coat the ball with a bit more Crisco, and wrap it tightly in plastic food wrap. Let sit for 30 minutes prior to use.

*Recipe from: **The Snarky Sweet Cake Chick***

Homemade Extracts

Have you recently bought a tiny jar of vanilla from the grocery store? Yikes, it's expensive. But did you know you can make your own vanilla extract, and, if kept properly, it can be kept for years to come? The famous Chef Ina Garten created her vanilla 20+ years ago. You can also make other extracts such as lemon, lime, orange, chocolate, almond, and cinnamon! Included here are some of my favorites.

Vanilla

- 1 cup of vodka (Most affordable, the brand name doesn't matter)
- 3 vanilla beans (Grade B)
- 1 Mason jar

Directions:

Pour one cup of vodka into Mason jar. With a sharp knife, cut the beans in half and then split the vanilla beans down the middle. Pop in Mason jar with the vodka and make sure the beans are covered in alcohol. (If beans aren't covered and are exposed to air, you're subject to having mold grow —ew.) Give it a few shakes and store in cool, dark cupboard. Shake your jar once a day for the first week, then every two weeks after while it's "brewing." Some people suggest waiting two months before it's ready to use and others suggest waiting two years before it's ready! My suggestion is waiting at least six months or once you can smell the vanilla without the smell of alcohol.

To ensure that it lasts, make sure the beans are covered in alcohol. At least once a year, add in a new bean or two to introduce more vanilla flavor.

Thoughts:

The idea of homemade vanilla just makes my heart happy. Not only are you saving money, but you're making it from scratch. This makes an adorable gift for any time of the year; just remember to start it early! As you probably already know, vanilla is a staple in every kitchen and its uses are endless!

Lemon

- 1 cup of vodka (Most affordable, the brand name doesn't matter)
- 3 lemons, washed and dry
- 1 Mason jar

Directions:

Pour one cup of vodka in Mason jar. With a fruit peeler, cut the rind off the lemon making sure not to get the white pith. Place beautiful yellow rinds in the Mason jar with vodka and give it a shake. Store in cool, dark cupboard. Shake your jar once a day for the first week, then every two weeks after while it's "brewing." This should be ready to use in about two months and should last for about one year. Keep stored in air-tight container in dark, cool cupboard.

Thoughts:

The zingy smell of lemon adds a dash of flavor and even larger dash of happy! As this one is brewing, I invite you to open the lid, close your eyes and inhale happily! Even if you never use this as an extract, you can certainly use it as a mood lifter.

It's this recipe that I use to make lime, orange, chocolate, almond, and cinnamon extracts.

"Paisley" Rolling Pin Design

Homemade Spice Blends

Much like making your homemade vanilla, you can do the same with your spice blends. Yes, you could buy these at the store but by making them at home you save some money and are able to use your own concoction in your baking as well as give these away as gifts.

Apple Pie Spice

- ½ cup cinnamon
- 1 tbsp nutmeg
- 1 tbsp allspice
- 1 tsp ginger

Pumpkin Pie Spice

- ½ cup cinnamon
- 4 tbsp ginger
- 1 tbsp allspice
- 1 tbsp nutmeg
- 1 tbsp cloves

*Recipes compliments of **The Domestic Geek.***

Variations·

After a few years of using the same cookie recipe, I got a bit bored. A whole new world opened up for me when I decided to play around with items I actually have at my fingertips. Below are some basics as well as fun ideas on how to add some fun into your creations.

Andes Mints

Melt a few of these yummies and fold into your wet ingredients. You'll get a wonderful peppermint taste. Or, drizzle over a cooled cookie for a fun decoration and yummy taste.

Melting Wafers

We seem to have chocolate everywhere in our house. One day I found a bag of chocolate melting wafers and wondered if I could incorporate them with our cookies. Well, I melted the chocolate and dipped in a baked shortbread cookie. It immediately changed the look of the cookie as well as added some sugary sweetness. This can also be used for décor as well as taste. Try the Chocolate Chipotle recipe and dip these dark cookies in vanilla chocolate and you've created the look of a black-and white-cookie.

Cinnamon

By adding in this dark spice, the dough turns just a smidge darker in color, which gives the dough some contrast. By adding in just a small amount (even just 2 tsp), your cookies will have some depth and make the impression appear stronger. Plus, cinnamon - yum!

Earl Grey Tea Leaves

Cut a tea bag and add the leaves to the dough for a slight flavor enhancement. Add to wet or dry ingredients. I even used Raspberry Zinger from the brand Celestial Seasoning, and not only did the cookies look delicious, but they also tasted fantastic!

Food Coloring

This is the part I love—adding in color. I leave this part to our daughter who always comes up with wonderful color creations. You can use store-bought food coloring or make your own. My favorite brand is Wilson Food Coloring.

Lemon Peel

Lemon adds happiness! Well, actually it adds the taste and scent of lemon, which means spring, flowers, and all things wonderful! I like to add the zest of 1 lemon (washed and dried) to my lemon-themed cookies. Add in with wet ingredients.

Hot Chocolate & Apple Cider packets

Stroll down the beverage aisle at the grocery store, and you'll see a variety of hot chocolate packets you can add to your dough. Dark chocolate, butterscotch, French vanilla, etc. Measure out the hot chocolate powder and simply decrease the flour the recipe calls for. The same principle applies to the apple cider packets.

LorAnn Oils Extracts and Emulsions

This is an online shop dedicated to all things extracts, emulsions, and baking fun! I love the Lemon and Orange Emulsions as well as the Red Velvet. Emulsions are stronger than extracts, don't bake out when baked, and are usually what I reach for first when I want to flavor a dough.

Luster Dust

This food-safe, mica powder can change the look of a cookie in a heartbeat! They can be found at your local craft store or online. Grab a small dish, 1 tsp of vodka, and add in the color you wish. Mix it up with a spoon and with fine tip paintbrush, "paint" the color onto the cookies.

Maple Syrup

While I love me some vanilla, it's getting really expensive. In lieu of vanilla, add maple syrup in the same increment.

Orange Peel

Orange adds happiness, too! I like to use the zest of 1 orange (washed and dried) to my cookies. Add in with wet ingredients.

Sanding Sugar

You can buy sanding sugar online or even make your own. My neighbor told me about this idea and it's genius. Grab a small container, add 1/4-cup sugar and a few drops of food coloring. Put the lid on and shake, shake, shake. Voila, homemade sanding sugar. As the cookies come out of the oven and are still hot, sprinkle sugar over the cookie.

Sprinkles

Sprinkles added to the top of a cookie create a festive look. Did you know you can also add sprinkles into your dough as well? It will add some texture and small pops of color.

Vanilla Bean

Interchangeable to using vanilla.

Vanilla Extract

Interchangeable to using vanilla bean extract.

Potential Problems
AND Common Questions

◆ *The dough keeps sticking to the pin.*

Re-dust your rolling pin with more flour before each pass. You can never use too much flour. Pretend you're painting the flour onto the rolling pin and cover every wood surface. I prefer using a pastry brush for this step.

◆ *I followed the recipe but the dough looks crumbly.*

It's important to use butter the way the recipe calls for it. Most recipes call for room temperature. If you see dough that looks more like crumbles then you most likely used butter that was too cold. To remedy this, simply add 1 tsp of water to the dough until it begins to resemble less clumpy dough.

◆ *I can see flour used from the rolling pin on top of the cookie itself.*

Not to worry. Just take a pastry brush and wipe off the excess flour when the cookie is cooled.

◆ *My baked cookies are super puffy and I can barely see the image.*

This happens if you over-mix the dough, specifically when you're creaming the eggs and sugar. Eggs are a binding agent as well as a leavener, and over-mixing will cause unwanted air in the dough, resulting in a puffed up cookie.

◆ *The impressions aren't showing up in the dough.*

You'll get better impressions if you bypass using the rolling pin handles and roll the barrel with the palms of your hands. This takes a bit of practice. If you're using a different recipe not included in this book, remove the leavening agents such as baking soda or baking powder. Both ingredients cause the cookie to puff up and potentially lose their image. (Recipes that call for leavening agents are typically not recommended.)

◆ *The tops of the cookies are cracked.*

Make sure you refrigerate your dough before it hits the oven. I actually refrigerate my dough twice. After I make the dough I flatten it, shape it into a disc, wrap it in plastic wrap, and put in fridge for 30 minutes. Then I roll it out, cut my shapes, and put it back in the fridge on a cookie sheet for 30 minutes.

◆ When I roll out the dough, a small bubble or pocket of air creeps up.

That usually means you rolled the dough too thin. You can either gently pat it down flat again or re-roll the dough.

◆ *Cookies are under baked or over baked but I followed the recipe.*

Every oven varies a smidge, so you may have to fiddle around with the oven's temperature until you find the sweet spot. I remove my cookies the moment the sides begin to brown. If your cookies are under baked, pop them back into the over until you see the sides begin to brown. You can always purchase an oven thermometer for your oven's accuracy.

◆ *I'm gluten free, now what?*

You can substitute various flour types to accommodate your tummy. In trying cookies with various flours, we found the cookies made with gluten-free flours to be quite crumbly.

◆ *I'm allergic to eggs.*

We substituted the Bob's Red Mill egg replacer and you couldn't detect a difference. You can also try a shortbread cookie, which typically is egg free.

◆ *We live at high altitude.*

Add in an additional 2 tbsp of flour.

◆ *I found another recipe I want to try; how will I know it will work?*

Finding new recipes to try is so fun and creative, and I encourage you to try as many as possible. Wouldn't it be fun to take an old family recipe and bring it back to life again? When reviewing other recipes, make sure the recipe doesn't call for large quantities of baking soda or baking powder. Both these leavening agents encourage the cookie to rise, which potentially means you lose the image of the cookie. Compare the ingredients listed in the recipes in this cookbook to see what's similar versus what's different. I'd say that if the recipe calls for less than 1 tsp of either ingredient, give it a shot!

◆ *I thought I could use these for pie crusts.*

Well, so did we. Some bakers say our sweet rolling pins can be used in homemade pie crusts if it's a shortbread-based recipe. Another option is to use the roll-out pie crusts from the grocery store. But because neither the homemade pie crust nor store-bought pie crusts worked 100% with our rolling pins (in our opinion), we can't say our pins work great. But if you're an overachiever and after reading this disclaimer you want to find or create a homemade pie crust...we'd LOVE to hear about it!

"Aspen Leaves" Rolling Pin

Resources

1. LorAnn Oils
   Online shop that features essential oils, candy oils, baking flavors, extracts, candy molds and supplies for candy making, baking and aromatherapy.
   www.lorannoils.com

2. The Cookie Cutter Shop
   Online shop that offers a variety of cookie cutters at great prices. Plus they have fun recipes that work with our Sweet Rolling Pins.
   www.thecookiecuttershop.com

3. Facebook groups:
   a. Molded Cookies of the World – Artisan Bakers and Confections
   b. The Springerle Cookie Appreciation Group

4. *Baking with Cookie Molds*, Anne L Wilson

5. *Top 50 Shortbread Recipes*, Julie Brooke

6. Pinterest: Molded Cookies, Springerle Cookies

7. When searching recipes use key words, "no spread cookie," "roll out cookie," or "molded cookie."

"Pine Cones & Mistletoe" Rolling Pin Design

Grandma Dorothy's Chocolate Pistacio Pie

Ingredients and Directions:

- Prepare pie shell (or purchase from store)
- 1 1/2 cups four
- 1/2 tsp salt

One fist size piece of shortening. Add enough water to make dough easy to handle. Do Not Roll. Press into large pie pan, shaping with fingers. Bake until brown at 450 oven. Pierce bottom with fork before baking.

Filling:

- 1 package dark chocolate pudding
- 1 small package instant Pistachio pudding
- 1/4 pint whipping cream
- 1 Tbsp powdered sugar
- 1/2 tsp vanilla
- 1 Hershey bar chilled

Prepare chocolate pudding and pour into cooled pie shell. After 30 minutes pour prepared pistachio pudding on top and chill. Then top with whipping cream. Shave chocolate bar on top.

Person in family who loved this most: Papa

"Milk Says the Cow" Rolling Pin Design

Conclusion

I hope you have found this recipe book both helpful and fun. Who did you bake with? What did you share about yourself as you decorated the cookies?

We're always on the lookout for more recipes to share with the world. Do you have one in mind that worked well with our engraved rolling pins? If so, we'd love to hear about it. If you would like to submit your recipe for our next book, we'd be grateful to hear from you. Please email to: recipes@ sweetrollingpins.com.

More importantly, if you have a story about how baking has enhanced your life or become a new passion we'd love to hear those stories as well. If you would like to submit your stories for an upcoming project we'd love to hear from you. Please email to: bakingstories@sweetrollingpins.com.

If you're into social media, follow us along our rolling pin journey as well as tag us with your fun cookie creations!

IG: @sweetrollingpins.com
FB: sweetrollingpins

Make Your Own Recipe

INGREDIENTS

INSTRUCTIONS

Make Your Own Recipe

INGREDIENTS

Make Your Own Recipe

INGREDIENTS

RECIPE

Flour

VANILLA extract

INSTRUCTIONS

"Camping Fun" - Engraved Rolling Pin Design

Coloring Pages for Little or Bored Bakers

Coloring Pages for Little or Bored Bakers

"Li'l Birdies" - Engraved Rolling Pin Design

Coloring Pages for Little or Bored Bakers

Coloring Pages for Little or Bored Bakers

"Nature Loving Kitties" - Engraved Rolling Pin Design

Coloring Pages for Little or Bored Bakers

CPSIA information can be obtained
at www.ICGtesting.com
Printed in the USA
FSHW011154121220
76688FS